Diabetic Juicing Recipes Cookbook:

Healthy and Easy Diabetic Juicing Diet.

By
Viktoria McCartney

Copyright [Viktoria McCartney]

Contents

Introduction

Have you ever wondered how something as simple as what you drink can profoundly impact your health? Health is a treasure we all cherish, and it often takes just a few mindful choices to maintain and even enhance it. When you take a sip of your favorite beverage, are you aware of how it might affect your body, especially if you are one of the millions of individuals living with diabetes?

Diabetes is a condition that affects people across the globe, challenging them to make conscious decisions about their diet and lifestyle. It demands a level of discipline and attention that can sometimes seem overwhelming. But it's also an opportunity to take charge of your health in a way that can lead to a vibrant and fulfilling life.

In this book, we will delve into a subject that is not only delicious but also essential for those managing diabetes: diabetic juices. We will explore how the juices you consume can significantly impact your well-being and how they can be customized to cater to your unique needs and preferences.

Why is Diet Crucial for Diabetic Patients?

Before we dive into the world of diabetic juices, let's take a moment to understand why diet is so crucial for those living with diabetes. Diabetes is a condition that affects the way your body processes glucose, which is the main source of energy for your cells. When this process goes awry, it can lead to high blood sugar levels, which can have serious health consequences.

Your diet plays a central role in managing these blood sugar levels. What you eat (or drink) directly affects how your body processes glucose. This means that choosing the right foods and beverages can help you keep your blood sugar within a healthy range, preventing complications associated with diabetes.

It's not just about saying no to sugary treats, although that's certainly a part of it. It's about making informed choices that balance carbohydrates, fats, and proteins while paying attention to portion sizes. And regarding beverages, what you drink can be just as important as what you eat.

The Power of Juices

Now, you might be wondering, "Why juices?" Well, juices are a fantastic addition to a diabetic's diet for several reasons. First and foremost, they are incredibly easy to prepare. All it takes is some fresh ingredients, a good juicer, and a dash of creativity, and you can whip up a delicious and nutritious beverage in no time.

Another remarkable quality of juices is their ability to keep you hydrated. Proper hydration is vital for everyone, but it's especially important for individuals with diabetes. Dehydration can lead to spikes in blood sugar levels, making it crucial to maintain a healthy fluid balance. Juices can help you achieve this while providing your body with essential vitamins, minerals, and antioxidants.

Diabetic Friendly Ingredients

Creating diabetic-friendly juices can be a flavorful and nutritious way to manage blood sugar levels. Here's a selection of fruits and vegetables that are excellent choices for crafting juices that won't cause rapid spikes in blood sugar:

Berries: Blueberries, strawberries, raspberries, and blackberries are rich in antioxidants, fiber, and vitamins. Their natural sweetness enhances the taste of your juice without causing a significant sugar rush.

Citrus Fruits: Oranges, grapefruits, lemons, and limes are low in sugar and provide a tangy flavor. They are also loaded with vitamin C, which can benefit overall health.

Leafy Greens: Spinach, kale, collard greens, and Swiss chard are low-carb, nutrient-packed additions to your juices. They offer vitamins, minerals, and antioxidants while helping to stabilize blood sugar levels.

Cucumber: Cucumbers are hydrating and have a mild, refreshing taste. They're low in carbohydrates, making them an ideal base for diabetic-friendly juices.

Celery: Celery is another low-carb vegetable that adds a crisp, clean flavor to your juices. It's high in fiber and can help control blood sugar.

Bell Peppers: These colorful vegetables provide a unique sweetness and are low in carbs. Bell peppers are rich in vitamins A and C, supporting a balanced diet.

Cinnamon: While not a fruit or vegetable, ground cinnamon is a fantastic spice to enhance flavor without adding sugar. It may also have potential benefits for blood sugar control.

Incorporating these diabetic-friendly fruits and vegetables into your juice recipes allows you to enjoy a wide range of flavors while keeping your blood sugar in check. Remember to consult with a healthcare professional or registered dietitian to create juices that align with your specific dietary needs and health goals.

Customizing Juices to Your Needs

One of the most exciting aspects of incorporating juices into your diet as a person with diabetes is the ability to customize them to your unique needs. You see, there's no one-size-fits-all approach to managing diabetes. Each person's body responds differently to various foods and beverages, and that's where the beauty of customization comes in.

With the right guidance and experimentation, you can tailor your juices to suit your dietary requirements. Whether you need to control your carbohydrate intake, increase your fiber intake, or focus on certain nutrients, you can create juices that align with your goals.

So, are you ready to begin this flavorful and nutritious journey with us? Together, we'll learn how to prepare diabetic juices that satisfy your taste buds and support your well-being. Prepare to sip your way to better health, one delicious glass at a time.

Strawberry Juice

Prep time: 10 minutes | Serves: 2 | Per Serving: Calories 46, Carbs 11.1g, Fat 0.4g, Protein 1g

Ingredients:

- Fresh strawberries – 2 C. hulled
- Fresh lime juice – 1 tsp.
- Filtered water – 2 C.

Directions:

1) Put the strawberries, lime juice, and water into a high-power blender process to form a smooth mixture.
2) Through a fine mesh strainer, strain the juice into glasses and enjoy immediately.

Cranberry Juice

Prep time: 10 minutes |Serves: 2 | Per Serving: Calories 148, Carbs 31.8g, Fat 0.2g, Protein 0.4g

Ingredients:

- Fresh cranberries – 2 C.
- Filtered water – ½ C.
- Fresh orange juice – ½ C.
- Fresh lemon juice – ½ tbsp.
- Liquid stevia – 3-4 drops

Directions:

1) Put the cranberries, water, orange juice, lemon juice, and liquid stevia into a high-power blender process to form a smooth mixture.
2) Through a fine mesh strainer, strain into glasses and enjoy immediately.

Blackberry Juice

Prep time: 10 minutes |Serves: 2 | Per Serving: Calories 111, Carbs 26.8g, Fat 0.3g, Protein 1.8g

Ingredients:

- Fresh blackberries – 4 oz.
- Seedless red grapes – 5 oz.
- Fresh mint leaves – 1 tbsp.
- Fresh lime juice – ½ tbsp.
- Filtered water – ¾ C.
- Liquid stevia – 3-4 drops

Directions:

1) Put the blackberries, grapes, mint leaves, lime juice, and water into a high-power blender process to form a smooth mixture.
2) Through a fine mesh strainer, strain the juice into glasses and blend in stevia. Enjoy immediately.

Mixed Berries Juice

Prep time: 10 minutes |Serves: 2 | Per Serving: Calories 247, Carbs 61.8g, Fat 1.7g, Protein 3.5g

Ingredients:

- Fresh blackberries – 1¼ C.
- Fresh blueberries – 1¼ C.
- Fresh raspberries – 1¼ C.
- Large-sized apples – 2, cored and sliced

Directions:

1) Put the berries and apples into a juicer and extract the juice according to the manufacturer's instructions.
2) Enjoy immediately.

Grape Juice

Prep time: 10 minutes │Serves: 2 │ Per Serving: Calories 63, Carbs 16.2g, Fat 0.3g, Protein 0.6g

Ingredients:

- Seedless red grapes – 2 C.
- Lime – ½, peeled
- Filtered water – 2 C.

Directions:

1) Put the grapes, lime, and water into a high-power blender process to form a smooth mixture.
2) Through a fine mesh strainer, strain the juice into glasses. Enjoy immediately.

Pomegranate Juice

Prep time: 10 minutes | Serves: 2 | Per Serving: Calories 63, Carbs 15g, Fat 0g, Protein 0.7g

Ingredients:

- Fresh pomegranate seeds – 1 C.
- Fresh lemon juice – 2 tsp.
- Filtered water – 1½ C.

Directions:

1) Put the pomegranate seeds, lemon juice, and water into a high-power blender process to form a smooth mixture.
2) Through a fine mesh strainer, strain the juice into glasses and enjoy immediately.

Pomegranate & Apple Juice

Prep time: 10 minutes | Serves: 2 | Per Serving: Calories 210, Carbs 53.2g, Fat 0.4g, Protein 1.6g

Ingredients:

- Fresh pomegranate seeds – 1½ C.
- Large-sized granny smith apples – 2, cored and sliced
- Fresh lemon juice – 2 tsp.
- Salt – 1 pinch
- Ground black pepper – 1 pinch

Directions:

1) Put pomegranate seeds and remnant ingredients into a juicer and extract the juice according to the manufacturer's instructions.
2) Enjoy immediately.

Plum Juice

Prep time: 10 minutes |Serves: 2 | Per Serving: Calories 91, Carbs 24.5g, Fat 0.6g, Protein 1.6g

Ingredients:

- Ripe plums – 6, pitted and cut up
- Lemon – ½, peeled
- Filtered water – 1 C.

Directions:

1) Put plums, lemon, and water into a high-power blender process to form a smooth mixture.
2) Through a fine mesh strainer, strain the juice into glasses and enjoy immediately.

Peach Juice

Prep time: 10 minutes │ Serves: 3 │ Per Serving: Calories 119, Carbs 28.3g, Fat 0.8g, Protein 2.8g

Ingredients:

- Medium-sized peaches – 6, peeled, pitted, and cut up
- Chilled filtered water – 2 C.
- Fresh lime juice – 1 tbsp.

Directions:

1) Put peaches and remnant ingredients into a high-power blender process to form a smooth mixture.
2) Through a fine mesh strainer, strain the juice into glasses and blend in stevia.
3) Enjoy immediately.

Apple Juice

Prep time: 10 minutes |Serves: 2 | Per Serving: Calories 241, Carbs 66.1g, Fat 0g, Protein 0g

Ingredients:

- Medium-sized granny smith apples – 6, cored and sliced
- Fresh lime juice – 1 tbsp.

Directions:

1) Put apples into a juicer and extract the juice according to the manufacturer's instructions.
2) Blend in lime juice and enjoy immediately.

Papaya Juice

Prep time: 10 minutes | Serves: 2 | Per Serving: Calories 90, Carbs 22.8g, Fat 0.4g, Protein 0.7g

Ingredients:

- Ripe papaya – 2 C. peeled, seeded, and cut up
- Fresh lemon juice – 1 tbsp.
- Filtered water – ½-¾ C.
- Liquid stevia – 3-4 drops

Directions:

1) Put the papaya, lemon juice, and water into a high-power blender process to form a smooth mixture.
2) Through a fine mesh strainer, strain the juice into glasses and blend in stevia.
3) Enjoy immediately.

Watermelon Juice

Prep time: 10 minutes |Serves: 2 | Per Serving: Calories 91, Carbs 22.8g, Fat 0.4g, Protein 1.8g

Ingredients:

- Small-sized watermelon – 1, peeled, seeded, and cut into Large-sized chunks
- Lemon – 1, peeled and seeded

Directions:

1) Put the watermelon and lemon into a juicer and extract juice per the manufacturer's instructions.
2) Enjoy immediately.

Grapefruit Juice

Prep time: 10 minutes │Serves: 2 │ Per Serving: Calories 120, Carbs 27.8g, Fat 0.2g, Protein 1.2g

Ingredients:

- Grapefruits – 3, peeled and sectioned
- Liquid stevia – 3-4 drops
- Filtered water – 1 C.

Directions:

1) Put the grapefruit sections and water into a high-power blender process to form a smooth mixture.
2) Through a fine mesh strainer, strain the juice into glasses and blend in stevia.
3) Enjoy immediately.

Orange Juice

Prep time: 10 minutes │Serves: 2 │ Per Serving: Calories 259, Carbs 64.9g, Fa*
0.7g, Protein 5.2g

Ingredients:

- Medium-sized oranges – 6, peeled and sectioned

Directions:

1) Put oranges into a juicer and extract the juice according to the manufacturer's instructions.
2) Enjoy immediately.

Pumpkin Juice

Prep time: 10 minutes | Serves: 2 | Per Serving: Calories 208, Carbs 54.5g, Fat 0.8g, Protein 2.2g

Ingredients:

- Pumpkin – 2 C. peeled, seeded, and cut into chunks
- Red apples – 3, cored and sliced
- Fresh ginger – 1 (½-inch) piece, peeled

Directions:

1) Put the pumpkin, apples, and ginger into a juicer and extract the juice according to the manufacturer's instructions.
2) Enjoy immediately.

Beet Juice

Prep time: 10 minutes | Serves: 2 | Per Serving: Calories 200, Carbs 45.2g, Fat 0.8g, Protein 7.6g

Ingredients:

- Beets – 2 lb. peeled and cut up
- Filtered water – ¼ C.

Directions:

1) Put beets and water into a high-power blender process to form a smooth mixture.
2) Through a fine mesh strainer, strain the juice into glasses and enjoy immediately.

Orange & Carrot Juice

Prep time: 10 minutes │Serves: 4 │ Per Serving: Calories 266, Carbs 56.6g, Fat 0.4g, Protein 5.3g

Ingredients:

- Carrots – 1 lb. peeled and roughly cut up
- Large-sized oranges – 4
- Fresh ginger – ¼ C.

Directions:

1) Put the carrots, ginger, and oranges into a juicer and extract the juice according to the manufacturer's instructions.
2) Enjoy immediately.

Carrot Juice

Prep time: 10 minutes | Serves: 2 | Per Serving: Calories 118, Carbs 28.3g, Fat 0g, Protein 2.4g

Ingredients:

- Large-sized carrots – 8, peeled and cut up
- Salt – 1 pinch
- Ground black pepper – 1 pinch

Directions:

1) Put carrots into a juicer and extract the juice according to the manufacturer's instructions.
2) Blend in salt and pepper and enjoy immediately.

Carrot & Ginger Juice

Prep time: 10 minutes | Serves: 2 | Per Serving: Calories 118, Carbs 28.3g, Fat 0g, Protein 2.4g

Ingredients:

- Large-sized carrots – 8, peeled and roughly cut up
- Lemon – 1, peeled and seeded
- Fresh ginger – ¼ C. peeled and sliced

Directions:

1) Put the carrots, lemon, and ginger into a juicer and extract the juice according to the manufacturer's instructions.
2) Enjoy immediately.

Apple & Carrot Juice

Prep time: 10 minutes │Serves: 2 │ Per Serving: Calories154, Carbs 39.8g, Fat 0.4g, Protein 1.4g

Ingredients:

- Large-sized carrots – 3, peeled and cut up
- Large-sized granny smith apples – 2, cored and sliced
- Salt – 1 pinch
- Ground black pepper – 1 pinch

Directions:

1) Put carrots and remnant ingredients into a juicer and extract the juice according to the manufacturer's instructions.
2) Blend in salt and pepper and enjoy immediately.

Beets, Carrots & Turmeric Juice

Prep time: 10 minutes │Serves: 6 │ Per Serving: Calories 174, Carbs 9. g, Fat 0.7g, Protein 5.1g

Ingredients:

- Large-sized carrots – 10, peeled and roughly cut up
- Large-sized golden beets – 6, peeled and roughly cut up
- Large-sized oranges – 2, peeled, seeded and sectioned
- Fresh turmeric – 1 (1-inch) piece, peeled and cut up

Directions:

1) Put carrots and remnant ingredients into a juicer and extract the juice according to the manufacturer's instructions.
2) Enjoy immediately.

Orange, Carrots & Beets Juice

Prep time: 10 minutes |Serves: 6 | Per Serving: Calories 204, Carbs 51.4g, Fat 0.6g, Protein 3.2g

Ingredients:

- Large-sized carrots – 10, peeled and roughly cut up
- Large-sized red beets – 10, peeled and roughly cut up
- Large-sized orange – 1, peeled and sectioned
- Lemon – 1, peeled and seeded
- Fresh ginger – ¼ C. peeled and cut up

Directions:

1) Put carrots and remnant ingredients into a juicer and extract the juice according to the manufacturer's instructions.
2) Enjoy immediately.

Orange, Carrot & Celery Juice

Prep time: 10 minutes | Serves: 2 | Per Serving: Calories 139, Carbs 33.5g, Fat 0.4g, Protein 3g

Ingredients:

- Celery stalks with leaves – 4
- Medium-sized carrots – 3, peeled and cut up
- Large-sized oranges – 2, peeled and sectioned
- Fresh ginger – 1 tbsp. peeled

Directions:

1) Put celery and remnant ingredients into a high-power blender process to form a smooth mixture.
2) Through a fine mesh strainer, strain the juice into glasses and enjoy immediately.

Red Fruit & Veggie Juice

Prep time: 10 minutes |Serves: 2 | Per Serving: Calories 258, Carbs 13.7g, Fat 1.8g, Protein 5.7g

Ingredients:

- Red beets – 2, peeled and roughly diced
- Large-sized red bell pepper – 1, seeded and cut up
- Large-sized tomato – 1, seeded and cut up
- Large-sized red apples – 2, cored and sliced
- Fresh strawberries – 2½ C. hulled and sliced
- Fresh mint leaves – ¼ C.

Directions:

1) Put beets and remnant ingredients into a juicer and extract juice per the manufacturer's instructions.
2) Enjoy immediately.

Tomato Juice

Prep time: 10 minutes | Serves: 2 | Per Serving: Calories 44, Carbs 9.6g, Fat 0.5g, Protein 2.2g

Ingredients:

- Medium-sized Fresh tomatoes – 4, cut up
- Chilled filtered water – ½ C.
- Salt – 1 pinch
- Ground black pepper – 1 pinch

Directions:

1) Put tomato pieces into a high-power blender process to form a smooth mixture.
2) Put in water, salt, and pepper and process to incorporate thoroughly.
3) Through a fine mesh strainer, strain the juice into glasses and enjoy immediately.

Apple, Spinach & Cucumber Juice

Prep time: 15 minutes | Serves: 6 | Per Serving: Calories 96, Carbs 22.9g, Fat 0.6g, Protein 4.1g

Ingredients:

- Large-sized cucumbers – 2, roughly cut up
- Large-sized granny smith apples – 2, cored and cut up
- Lime – 1, peeled, halved and seeds removed
- Fresh ginger – ¼ C. peeled and cut up
- Fresh spinach – 3 C.

Directions:

1) Put the cucumbers, ginger, lime, and apples into a juicer and extract juice according to the manufacturer's instructions.
2) Place extracted juice into a blender with spinach and blend until smooth.
3) Through a fine mesh strainer, strain the juice into glasses.
4) Enjoy immediately.

Cucumber & Celery Juice

Prep time: 10 minutes |Serves: 2 | Per Serving: Calories 113, Carbs 26.7g, Fat 0.6g, Protein 3.8g

Ingredients:

- Large-sized cucumbers – 2, roughly cut up
- Celery stalks – 6, roughly cut up
- Fresh ginger – ¼ C. peeled and sliced
- Large-sized oranges – 2, peeled, seeded and sectioned
- Lemon – 1, peeled and seeded

Directions:

1) Put cucumbers and remnant ingredients into a juicer and extract juice per the manufacturer's method.
2) Enjoy immediately.

Zucchini Juice

Prep time: 10 minutes |Serves: 2 | Per Serving: Calories 176, Carbs 43.2g, Fat 1.2g, Protein 4.2g

Ingredients:

- Zucchinis – 1¼ lb. roughly cut up
- Green apples – 2, cored and sliced
- Kiwi fruits – 2, peeled and roughly cut up
- Fresh ginger – 1 (1-inch) piece, peeled and cut up
- Fresh mint leaves – ¼ C.

Directions:

1) Put zucchini and remnant ingredients into a juicer and extract the juice according to the manufacturer's instructions.
2) Enjoy immediately.

Aloe Vera Juice

Prep time: 10 minutes | Serves: 2 | Per Serving: Calories 139, Carbs 33.6g, Fat 0.5g, Protein 1.7g

Ingredients:

- Small-sized aloe vera leaf – 1
- Fresh orange juice – 2 C.
- Liquid stevia – 5-6 drops

Directions:

1) With a sharp knife, peel the skin of the leaf.
2) Then remove the yellow layer just beneath the rind and discard it.
3) Place the aloe vera gel, orange juice, and maple syrup into a high-power blender process to form a smooth mixture.
4) Through a fine mesh strainer, strain the juice and enjoy immediately.

Apple, Kale & Cucumber Juice

Prep time: 10 minutes | Serves: 2 | Per Serving: Calories 229, Carbs 56.5g, Fat 0.8g, Protein 6.7g

Ingredients:

- Fresh kale – 4 C.
- Cucumbers – 2, cut up roughly
- Large-sized granny smith apples – 2, cored and sliced
- Large-sized lemon – 1, peeled and quartered

Directions:

1) Put kale and remnant ingredients into a juicer and extract the juice according to the manufacturer's instructions.
2) Enjoy immediately.

Kale, Cucumber & Parsley Juice

Prep time: 10 minutes | Serves: 2 | Per Serving: Calories 120, Carbs 26.5g, Fat 0.5g, Protein 6.5g

Ingredients:

- Fresh baby kale – 4 C.
- Large-sized seedless cucumbers – 2
- Fresh parsley – ½ C.
- Fresh ginger – 1 (1-inch) piece, peeled

Directions:

1) Put kale and remnant ingredients into a juicer and extract the juice according to the manufacturer's instructions.
2) Enjoy immediately.

Apple, Celery & Ginger Juice

Prep time: 10 minutes | Serves: 2 | Per Serving: Calories 242, Carbs 63.5g, Fat 0.9g, Protein 1.6g

Ingredients:

- Large-sized green apples – 4, cored and sliced
- Celery stalks – 5
- Fresh ginger – 1 (1-inch) piece, peeled

Directions:

1) Put apples and remnant ingredients into a juicer and extract the juice according to the manufacturer's instructions.
2) Enjoy immediately.

Greens, Celery & Carrot Juice

Prep time: 10 minutes | Serves: 2 | Per Serving: Calories 77, Carbs 16.7g, Fat 0.2g, Protein 4.1g

Ingredients:

- Fresh kale – 3 C.
- Fresh arugula – 2 C.
- Large-sized carrot – 1, peeled and cut up roughly
- Celery stalks – 2
- Lemon – 1
- Fresh ginger – 1 (1-inch) piece

Directions:

1) Put kale and remnant ingredients into a juicer and extract the juice according to the manufacturer's instructions.
2) Enjoy immediately.

Kale, Pear & Grapefruit Juice

Prep time: 10 minutes | Serves: 2 | Per Serving: Calories 198, Carbs 49.8g, Fat 0.5g, Protein 3.6g

Ingredients:

- Large-sized pears – 2, cored and sliced
- Grapefruits – 2, peeled
- Fresh kale – 2 C.
- Fresh ginger – 1 (1-inch) piece, peeled

Directions:

1) Put pears and remnant ingredients into a juicer and extract the juice according to the manufacturer's instructions.
2) Enjoy immediately.

Mixed Veggies Juice

Prep time: 10 minutes | Serves: 2 | Per Serving: Calories 89, Carbs 19.9g, Fat 0.4g, Protein 4.1g

Ingredients:

- Fresh kale – 2 C.
- Fresh tomatoes – 1 C.
- Large-sized carrot – 1, cut up
- Cucumber – 1, cut up
- Celery stalk – 1
- Fresh lime juice –2 tbsp.

Directions:

1) Put kale and remnant ingredients into a juicer and extract the juice according to the manufacturer's instructions.
2) Enjoy immediately.

Swiss Chard, Apple & Orange Juice

Prep time: 10 minutes |Serves: 2 | Per Serving: Calories 271, Carbs 69.8g, Fat 1g, Protein 3.6g

Ingredients:

- Swiss chard – 3 C.
- Apples – 3, cored and sliced
- Large-sized oranges – 2, peeled and sectioned

Directions:

1) Put Swiss chard and remnant ingredients into a juicer and extract the juice according to the manufacturer's instructions.
2) Enjoy immediately.

Apple, Celery & Cucumber Juice

Prep time: 10 minutes | Serves: 2 | Per Serving: Calories 167, 42.7g, 0.8g, Protein 2.8g

Ingredients:

- Large-sized apples – 2, cored and sliced
- Celery stalks – 4
- Medium-sized cucumber – 2

Directions:

1) Put apples and remnant ingredients into a juicer and extract the juice according to the manufacturer's instructions.
2) Enjoy immediately.

Pear, Kale & Celery Juice

Prep time: 10 minutes |Serves: 2 | Per Serving: Calories 250, Carbs 62.3g, 0.5g, Protein 5.3g

Ingredients:

- Pears – 4, cored and sliced
- Fresh kale – 4 C.
- Celery stalks – 2

Directions:

1) Put pears and remnant ingredients into a juicer and extract the juice according to the manufacturer's instructions.
2) Enjoy immediately.

Pear, Kale & Fennel Juice

Prep time: 10 minutes │Serves: 2 │ Per Serving: Calories 270, Carbs 67.4g, Fat 0.7g, 5.7g

Ingredients:

- Pears – 3, cored and sliced
- Fresh kale – 3 C.
- Fennel bulb – 1
- Fresh ginger – 1 (½-inch) piece, peeled

Directions:

1) Put pears and remnant ingredients into a juicer and extract the juice according to the manufacturer's instructions.
2) Enjoy immediately.

Apple, Carrot & Tomato Juice

Prep time: 10 minutes | Serves: 2 | Per Serving: Calories 162, Carbs 41.4g, Fat 0.6g, Protein 2g

Ingredients:

- Large-sized granny smith apples – 2, cored and sliced
- Large-sized tomato – 1, sliced
- Large-sized carrots – 2, peeled and cut up

Directions:

1) Put apples and remnant ingredients into a juicer and extract the juice according to the manufacturer's instructions.
2) Enjoy immediately.

Apple, Celery & Herbs Juice

Prep time: 10 minutes │Serves: 2 │ Per Serving: Calories 76, Carbs 18.7g g, Fat 0.5g, 1.2g

Ingredients:

- Granny Smith apple – 1, cored and sliced
- Celery stalks – 8
- Fresh parsley – ¼ C.
- Fresh cilantro – ¼ C.
- Fresh ginger – 1 (1-inch) piece
- Fresh lemon juice – 2 tsp.

Directions:

1) Put apple and remnant ingredients into a juicer and extract the juice according to the manufacturer's instructions.
2) Enjoy immediately.

Kale & Orange Juice

Prep time: 10 minutes │Serves: 2 │ Per Serving: Calories 282, Carbs 68.1g, Fat 0.6g, Protein 8.3g

Ingredients:

- Fresh kale – 4 C.
- Oranges – 5, peeled and sectioned

Directions:

1) Put kale and oranges into a juicer and extract the juice according to the manufacturer's instructions.
2) Enjoy immediately.

Kiwi, Apple & Grape Juice

Prep time: 10 minutes │Serves: 2 │ Per Serving: Calories 209, Carbs 52.7g, Fat 1g, Protein 2g

Ingredients:

- Large-sized kiwis – 4, peeled and cut up
- Large-sized green apple – 1, cored and sliced
- Seedless green grapes – 1 C.
- Fresh lime juice – 2 tsp.

Directions:

1) Put kiwis and remnant ingredients into a juicer and extract the juice according to the manufacturer's instructions.
2) Enjoy immediately.

Pears, Celery & Spinach Juice

Prep time: 10 minutes | Serves: 2 | Per Serving: Calories 209, Carbs 50.5g, Fat 0.9g, Protein 5.1g

Ingredients:

- Pears – 6, cored and cut up
- Celery stalks – 3
- Fresh spinach – 3 C.
- Fresh parsley –2 tbsp.

Directions:

1) Put pears and remnant ingredients into a juicer and extract the juice according to the manufacturer's instructions.
2) Enjoy immediately.

Apple, Pear & Spinach Juice

Prep time: 10 minutes |Serves: 2 | Per Serving: Calories 293, Carbs 74.6g, Fat 0.8g, Protein 4.6g

Ingredients:

- Large-sized green apples – 2, cored and sliced
- Large-sized pears– 2, cored and sliced
- Fresh spinach – 3 C.
- Celery stalks – 3
- Lemon – 1, peeled

Directions:

1) Put apples and remnant ingredients into a juicer and extract the juice according to the manufacturer's instructions.
2) Enjoy immediately.

Broccoli, Apple & Orange Juice

Prep time: 10 minutes | Serves: 2 | Per Serving: Calories 254, Carbs 64.7g, Fat 0.8g, Protein 3.8g

Ingredients:

- Broccoli stalks – 2, cut up
- Large-sized green apples – 2, cored and sliced
- Large-sized oranges – 3, peeled and sectioned
- Fresh parsley – 4 tbsp.

Directions:

1) Put broccoli and remnant ingredients into a juicer and extract the juice according to the manufacturer's instructions.
2) Enjoy immediately.

Gooseberry Juice

Prep time: 10 minutes | Serves: 2 | Per Serving: Calories15, Carbs 3.7g, Fat 0.2g, Protein 0.4g

Ingredients:

- Gooseberries – ¼ C. cut up
- Filtered water – 1 C.
- Lemon – 1, peeled
- Fresh ginger – 1 tsp. peeled and cut up
- Fresh mint leaves – 10
- Salt – 1 pinch
- Ground black pepper – 1 pinch

Directions:

1) Put gooseberries and remnant ingredients into a high-power blender process to form a smooth mixture. Through a fine mesh strainer, strain the juice into glasses and enjoy immediately.

Kale, Arugula & Apple Juice

Prep time: 10 minutes |Serves: 2 | Per Serving: Calories 113, Carbs 26.7g, Fat
0.6g, Protein 3.8g

Ingredients:

- Fresh kale – 5 oz.
- Fresh arugula – 2 oz.
- Fresh parsley – ¼ C.
- Celery stalks – 4
- Green apple – 1, cored and cut up
- Fresh ginger – 1 (1-inch) piece, peeled
- Lemon – 1, peeled

Directions:

1. Put kale and remnant ingredients into a juicer and extract the juice according to the manufacturer's instructions.
2. Enjoy immediately.

Celery Juice

Prep time: 10 minutes | Serves: 2 | Per Serving: Calories 33, Carbs 6.8g, Fat 0.5g, Protein 1.1g

Ingredients:

- Celery stalks with leaves – 8
- Fresh ginger – 2 tbsp. peeled
- Lemon – 1, peeled
- Filtered water – ½ C.
- Salt – 1 pinch

Directions:

1) Put celery and remnant ingredients into a high-power blender process to form a smooth mixture.
2) Through a fine mesh strainer, strain the juice into glasses and enjoy immediately.

Conclusion

In the world of juicing, finding that perfect, crave-worthy blend can be a delightful journey of experimentation and discovery. It takes a dash of effort, a sprinkle of creativity, and a willingness to try new ingredients to create juices that tantalize your taste buds while keeping your blood sugar in check. But it's more than just sipping on a tasty drink; juicing can also be a form of meditation. The act of carefully selecting and preparing ingredients, the soothing hum of the juicer, and the mindful savoring of each sip can create a moment of calm in our often-hectic lives. It's a chance to pause, reflect, and nourish our bodies and souls. So, whether you're new to juicing or a seasoned pro, remember that it's not just about what's in the glass; it's about the journey and the joy of sipping your way to better health and mindfulness. Cheers to your juicing adventure!

Printed in Great Britain
by Amazon

46360676R00034